UP UNTIL NOW

The 3 Magic Words That Stop Fear, Stress & Anxiety From Running Your Life.

Many Blessings on your path.
♡: Meagan
2016

Meagan McKerroll

DEDICATION

This book is dedicated to all of the people who are waking up from their deep sleep and recognizing that it's time for a change. To all of the people who don't think they have what it takes, think again! This one's for you!

TABLE OF CONTENTS

ACKNOWLEDGEMENTS

A huge acknowledgment goes out to my parents. Thank you for always embracing my wild heart, free spirit, and adventurous soul. Thank you for instilling in me the belief that anything is possible. I Love You.

A big thank you to all of the mentors, coaches, teachers, adventurers, healers, clients, and shamans that I have had the privilege to work with from around the world – words do no justify as to the depths of gratitude I hold for each and every one of you. Thank you for holding such sacred space for me to step into my becoming.

And last, but certainly not least, my profound gratitude goes out to the 'All One Primal Universal Source Energy' that lives and breathes me every single day. Without being plugged into you, none of this would be possible.

Eternal Gratitude! So Be It & So It Is.

TESTIMONIALS

"I just love your energy! Like a burst of Wonder and Joy."

- Tyrone Acevedo

"Meagan McKerroll is a world-class life coach who offers the kind of mentoring support you wished you had and you'll thank your lucky stars that you found her.... She has mastered that unbeatable and highly sought-after combination of listening caringly and responding intuitively, taking her clients and their most sought after dreams through quantum leaps and into inspired action..."

– Anne Perrah, Ph.D., Educator, Author,
Certified Life Coach & Heart-Centered Family Mentor

"I have been privileged enough to know Meagan for 4 years, and she is truly a 'once in a lifetime' individual..."

- Joshua Irvine, Sales & Management Professional

"You are just inspiring beyond words. The facts that both times I have seen you present has made me well up with tears goes to show how effective you are. Thank you Meg!"

- Catharine O'Leary

"... I love the emotional growth I feel in your sessions. I leave with nuggets of information that I ponder on for days afterwards. Thank so much!"

- Jenn Whyte

"You are a true healing Goddess. The End!"

- Sarah K.

"Thank you for opening up more of my world. It is always a joy to talk to you and learn more about myself."

- John Gribben

"Meagan is a talented, dynamic inspiring speaker. Her positive, passionate, energetic and motivational style puts her audience at ease and creates an environment where it's comfortable not just to think about your dream but believe in it! Meagan leaves her audience excited, empowered and ready to actualize success in all aspects of their lives."

-Julie Cayley, Independent Consultant & Entrepreneur

CHAPTER 1 - REMEMBERING

If there's one thing that I have learned in life it's that you can study, you can know, you can learn all that you can possibly learn, but it means nothing if you don't actually apply it and put it to use in your everyday life.

Being a walking encyclopedia of information and knowledge, or new age wisdom does not guarantee that a person will be prosperous, loved, or successful (in whatever way you define success to be in your life).

Knowing something out of a book versus actually applying it first hand in your life are two very different things, and yet, it is what I see people doing day in and day out; it's how I once lived my life too.

The sad truth is that when we see something on TV, hear something from a coach/mentor or overhear someone else speaking about a universal truth we automatically think we know it and therefore it will change our lives.

It's like watching the movie "The Secret" where they introduce you to The Law of Attraction and now you think that by simply seeing that movie your life is going to be more prosperous and joyful than ever before.

The truth is, unless you actually do something with what you are learning, hearing, seeing, etc.... nothing in your life will change. If you aren't able to demonstrate and put into action all of the knowledge that you've gained, you might as well be a book on a shelf.

We truly are Spiritual Beings here in a human body to grow and expand our consciousness, live and experience life, and apply and practice what we have been learning in order to return to our true authentic selves.

What most people don't know is that there is a place between these two worlds, the Spirit and the Human, and this place is where the veil is the thinnest. We are able to connect with our higher self so that we can fully acknowledge, and come into alignment with, the Infinite Intelligence that is living and breathing us right now.

It is this place where I wish to bring you. The pages of this book are filled with energy that will be transmuted to you as you begin to remember who you really are and why you're really here having this human experience we call LIFE.

For some of you, you already know this place well and yet you're still not sure of what to do when you get there; for others, it will be brand new! Either way, know that wherever you are in your life, right here and right now, it is divinely timed and in perfect alignment with the journey of your soul.

You are here for a reason and for a purpose, you just don't remember! You are much more than you think you are. You are much more than society has conditioned you to be. You are magnificent! You are powerful! And you are capable of having, being, doing, experiencing, giving and receiving all of the things that you have been merely dreaming about.

There is something magical happening within you that you are starting to feel, and everyone on the planet needs you to wake up, to remember, and to ignite the flame that dwells deep within your heart.

Your time is now!

Let the journey begin.

Here we go!

Notes

CHAPTER 2 - WHAT THE HECK HAPPENED?

"The journey of a thousand miles begins with a single step"

- Lao Tzu

The journey begins with us getting real about a few things, starting with a simple acknowledgment that we have all wanted to improve some aspect of our lives at one point or another to bring us more happiness. We have all wanted this! That's right, even you. It is our human nature.

Lately, however, it seems that so many people in the world are dreadfully unhappy, to the point where they hate their jobs, they hate their lives, they hate their mates, they hate their bodies, and they suffer from what I call the shiny ball syndrome. You know the one; it goes a little something like this:

"Hey, I don't know what to do with my life. I feel insecure and I don't fit in. I'm afraid to really be myself because of what other people might think of me, and I don't have the self-esteem or self-worth to actually say what I mean and stick up for myself so I'm just going to keep jumping and spinning and doing backflips for whoever gives me attention, and tells me what I should do."

The shiny ball shows up and you jump on it. Then another one pops up and you leave what you just started and run for something new hoping that it will fulfill you. Hoping that it will plug the empty whole in your heart. Hoping that it will love you in the way you yearn to be loved and seen.

When really, the only person who can fill that gaping whole, and who can love you, honor you, respect you, show up for you, make you happy, the whole 9 yards, is (wait for it).... YOU! Yes, the one and only YOU!

And yet, for many of us, looking inside and getting real with 'who we really are' is the last place in the world we want to look for our answers. Even with all of the unhappiness, fear, stress, overwhelm, anxiousness, and unresolved feelings that we are experiencing, we still want to look outside of ourselves for something to fix us.

Why is that?

Well, we live in a world that has been conditioning us since we were a very young age. We're taught to look a certain way, act a certain way, make a certain amount of money in order to be successful, think like everyone else, live from what the economy tells us, be afraid of things that are different, don't be too unique or different because then people won't like you and you won't fit in.

Whew, that's a mouthful, but it's true! Now, I don't know about you, but I'm at a stage in my life where I'm calling it! Yep! I call Bullshit! (Oops, can I write that? Haha, I just did!)

Seriously though, think about this for a minute. Since you were a young child you have always tried to do what? Fit In! And if you're really honest with yourself you've also been trying to do what? Be loved! Since you were a young child you have definitely been trying to live in a way that would get the approval and attention from the ones you loved the most.

And here's the thing! Since you were a young child you have been taught to look externally for all of your answers. You have been taught to go outside of yourself before you were ever taught to go INSIDE of yourself to experience the love, acceptance, peace, respect, honor, understanding, and attention you so deeply desire.

And what ends up happening to you along the way is very sad, because as a child you want to fit in so badly that you're willing to suppress the very essence of who you are in order to do so.

You're willing to put on the masks, put on the armor and get into this thing we call life so that you can show your family, your teachers, your peers, and the world just how perfect and amazing you really are. All the while, the real you, the TRUE YOU, is being pushed down deeper and deeper, never to see the light of day, drowning in sorrow that you aren't living your Soul's purpose so that coming into your later years of life you wonder why you're not happy.

"What the heck happened?" you ask yourself as you look around to see all of the 'stuff' that you've surrounded yourself with that 'society', 'other people' and 'the world' has told you will make you feel complete.

You thought that if you had: the house, the car, the 2.5 kids (it's true, this is the societal norm for happiness, don't ask me how you deal with that .5) the dog, the body, the career, the enviable salary, and the vacation house to escape to when life really gets hard, that you would be happy. When really, it couldn't be further from the truth!

And that's not all!

The saddest part of this whole thing is that that moment in life when you really were being yourself was also the moment where mom and dad didn't' agree, the teachers at school got uncomfortable with you, the person you were dating didn't seem to love you as much, and all of a sudden you decided, "hey, I guess I'm better off just being the person that everybody else likes." It felt wrong not to be accepted, so you did whatever you could to be accepted.

The point I'm trying to make here is that all of us have tried to be something that we're not in order to win the approval, love, and attention of the people closest to us because we were taught to look outside of ourselves for all of our answers.

We have forgotten that we are more than just our bodies. Our bodies are such an important part of our being'ness, but they are not everything. They are the vehicle, the vessel, and the conduit for our spirit to be here, living, breathing and sharing our unique gifts, talents, and light with the rest of the planet. Not just the people on this planet, the entire planet inclusive of the land, waters, plants and animals.

We have forgotten that we are unique and there will never be another person like us, like you, ever! Never ever!

We have forgotten that we live in an inside out Universe where the one place that we must go in order to have the things in our external world that we desire is, in fact, inside.

We have forgotten that the true source of happiness lives within us and that we are a part of the All One/Infinite Intelligence/Great Spirit/Primal Source Energy that gives life to the entire Universe.

We have forgotten that external things, although lovely to have, in the end, won't bring us the joy we seek if we aren't fulfilled and honest with who we really are from the inside out.

As a Spiritual Teacher, Author, and Speaker - it is my deepest intent to give you a very practical tool in this book to assist you with your journey to living in alignment with your Soul's true purpose. I am blessed to be in a position where I can share with you wisdom and insights passed down through the ages that will help you RIGHT NOW in your life if you will only commit to putting it into practice.

Before we begin you must know that you are here for a purpose and a reason and that you have certain gifts, talents and attributes that need to be shared with the world.

The key to living from this place, however, is to tap into the truth of 'who you really are' by being yourself and honoring your perfect imperfections and loving your quirky, wild, beautiful self. You must honor that the real you does exist and that you are much more than just a physical body that gets out of bed, goes to work, pays your taxes, eats, poops, tends to your family, and sleeps!

So how do you do this?

This is the million-dollar question that everyone in the world is looking for the answer to. Let me introduce you to the 3 magic words that will change your life forever. Get ready to stop all of the fear, all of the stress, and all of the anxiety that is keeping you from being YOU.

Those 3 magic words are.... ***UP UNTIL NOW***.

Up Until Now, you haven't been happy.

Up Until Now, you haven't been healthy.

Up Until Now, you haven't experienced financial freedom.

Up Until Now, you likely didn't even know there was another way to live your life.

Up Until Now, you have been living with feelings of fear, stress and anxiety when it comes to knowing what to do, where to go, how to do it and how to make it happen.

And now, written in the pages of this book, you are about to learn and explore the practical concepts and principles that will literally set you free from your old ways of living, and allow you to step into the light of who you truly are.

Living without fear, without crazy levels of stress, and without the anxiousness that is coursing throughout the world will, indeed, be a revelation in and of itself.

So I invite you to sit back, put your feet up, get comfortable, and above all else, TRUST that you are reading these words because your time has come and you are now ready to ignite the Spirit that dwells deep within your soul.

Let's roll baby!

CHAPTER 3 - WHAT YOU NEED TO KNOW!

"The world is but a canvas to our imagination"

- Henry David Thoreau

My life has not always been as it is right now. I wasn't always an author, or a speaker, or a healer, or a spiritual teacher guiding people back into themselves. In fact, I was quite the opposite. I was someone who was totally stuck in my head, completely driven by external circumstances and situations, and trying to fit into a world that really wasn't meant for me to fit into.

From a young age, I had been living my life in the fast lane! Travelling, living and working all over the world, competing as an athlete in various events and disciplines, eating whatever I wanted and drinking whatever I wanted with no regard for my body or what it needed to survive. I was being the best daughter, sister, girlfriend, co-worker and leader that I could be and I was doing it all while wearing a big mask and putting on layers of armor so that no one could see how much of a mess I was inside.

As a young girl, I had a lisp, so I couldn't pronounce S's, T's, P's, or C's. Looking back at it now, I fully understand why I needed to overcome that barrier of communication, but at the time, as you can fully imagine, it was not ok! It was not easy to be a young girl, who was also a tomboy in school with a lisp, who had to go to the special education teacher for private help. Yeah! You get it.

I was also in a place in my life where I didn't know that there was life beyond my body. So when the first of three knee surgeries came upon me and I was taken out of athletics, I was at a loss! I didn't know how to do anything other than to use my body to train, or ride, or dance, or run. I had no idea how to sit still with myself, nor did I want to.

Sitting still with yourself really sucks when you have no idea how to calm all of the nonsense going through your mind, and are being bombarded with outside stimulations from your environment to always be on the move and strive for something more.

On the Spiritual side, and I'll be very honest - I had no spiritual side, or so I thought. In those days, all I knew was that anything my mind could think, my body had to do, because that's what it had been doing.

Now at the same time, if you had been looking in on my life from the outside it looked really incredible. I was happy-go-lucky, with the perfect life, the perfect mate, the perfect body, the perfect job(s) and opportunities to do things that people only dreamt of, and yet, I was discontent and constantly searching for something, or someone, to fill my void and bring me peace and happiness.

It was one morning in the fall many years ago when I woke up to my body no longer being able to carry me on my crusade to be anybody but myself. I had been living my life for everyone else, and I had been doing it in a way that was so out of balance and full of anxiety and stress, that I actually led myself straight onto my deathbed at the young age of 23 years old.

So picture me, 23 years of age in the hospital, quarantined, alone and scared, weighing 90 pounds, with excruciating pain all over my body, dying! I remember thinking to myself, "This can't be it! I'm not ready to die yet, there's way too much life left to live and so many people who I still want to help. It can't be my time. This isn't the way I'm meant to go out!"

As you can imagine I was emotionally drained, mentally drained, physically drained, and it felt like there was no spirit in me left to be drained. All the while, it felt oddly peaceful to have death staring me right in the face with nowhere to hide, and for the first time, actually feeling like I was being seen.

After 3 weeks of hospital quarantine and watching myself slowly fade away to nothing, on the night of my birthday I recall dragging my frail body onto the cold hospital floor and having a talk with the Universe. This was something I had not done since a very young age, and I said, "Whatever the heck is out there, or whatever is up there, God! Or some kind of Spirit, whoever you are, I am not ready! I'm not meant to go yet! I need more time!"

I went on to say, "Listen up Universe!" (I was rather cocky back then, as if you say 'Listen Up Universe' to the Universe! I mean come on, who does that right? It's the freakin' Universe we're talking about here people).

Anyways, moving on, I said "Listen up Universe! If you let me live I will give you the best darn show that you've seen down here in a really long time! I promise that I will live my life authentically, and I promise that I will be open to living my life in a new and more empowered way if you just show me how. I've been doing this life all backwards and I can see that now, so get me out of this dreadful hospital, and let's figure this thing out."

I woke up the next morning, somehow in my bed, and knew it was time to get out of that hospital. Thankfully, I might add, I left with all of my organs, of which the doctors at the time not knowing what was wrong with me thought it might be a good idea to take out my pancreas, gallbladder, and 10 feet of my small intestines just to be safe. Needless to say, I rejected that absurd idea and got the heck out'a dodge!

Now I share this part of my story with you not as a 'come to Jesus moment' but rather to help illustrate how hard I had to push, how much I had to hurt, how far I had to go down the wrong path before I woke up to the truth and realized that there is something far more Divine happening in this world than just me and my body.

And I'm sure you can relate because at one point or another you have pushed, and forced, and done things that you thought we right for you based on what the outside world was telling you to do, only to really find out that it was hurting you in one way, shape or form.

So from that moment on I could no longer be a victim and neglect my body, my thoughts, my emotions, my feelings, or my dreams. I knew how important and fragile life was after that experience, and yet I had to almost kill myself in order to learn it.

If I wanted to stay and live and play and help people in this lifetime, I had to learn how to take care of this incredible vehicle that would be taking me through my journey, and so I did.

Over the course of many years, as I learned about the physical body, I also learned and worked in the area's of my emotional, mental, and spiritual bodies and became deeply passionate about exploring how interrelated and connected they all are.

The old story of who I was had to change. The life that I had once known had to go as I entered into a whole new world of alternative healing and medicine that was incredibly foreign to me.

I was met with alternative practices and therapies, new age philosophy's and teachings, began studying with shamans and other esoteric healers around the globe, and became trained in many different disciplines and modalities to promote growth, healing, transformation, and forward movement in my life and the lives of others.

I was blessed to study with some of the top coaches and mentors in the world when it came to personal growth, transformation, and spiritual development.

Along the way I had to make some big changes in my life. I had to change what I ate, I had to change what I thought, I had to change who I spent my time with, I had to leave a career, friends, old conveniences and the demands of the outside world in order to journey within and not only rediscover who I was, but ignite the flame in my heart that I had been constantly snuffing out because I was afraid.

I share this with you because as I write these words onto these pages, I need you to know that I've been there too.

I know how hard it can be to change. I know what it feels like to be scared. To not want to get out of bed, to just want to give up, to wish you were anyone other than who you are, and to want to change but not actually have to *do* anything for it.

I know what it feels like to not fit in. I know what it feels like to not have two pennies to rub together. I know what it feels like to hit rock bottom and think that you are alone in this world and you can't trust anyone or anything. I know what it feels like to have your heart torn out & crushed on the floor right in front of you.

I know shame, I know guilt, I know being a control freak, I know stress and worry and overwhelm and anxiety oh so well because I used to be just like you. Always concerned as to where the money was going to come from. Always trying to work so hard, 2 or 3 jobs, so that I could just make ends meet. I know what it feels like to live without any kind of connection to something greater because I did so for a long time before I woke up.

But I also know what it's like to surrender, to trust, to let go, to receive, to allow, and to be so plugged in and tuned in, that nothing in this world could take away the happiness, prosperity, and joy that resides within me.

I know you can relate to this or you would not be reading these words right now. I know there is a part of you just crying to be let out, and yet you're scared.

You're afraid that your friends won't like you anymore, you're afraid that your family will disown you, you're afraid that your partner in life will leave you and find someone else. You're afraid that you're not good enough, you're not smart enough, you're not pretty enough, you're not rich enough, you're not tall enough, and you're sure as heck not stable enough to be your true self. That is, *Up Until Now*!

These 3 magical words will assist you through the unchartered waters ahead so that you can begin living with more courage, more confidence, and more peace in your life than ever before.

Notes

CHAPTER 4 - CHANGING THE CHANNEL

"You will never do great things in the external world until you think great things in the internal world"

- Wallace Wattles

These life-changing words, *Up Until Now*, were introduced to me by one of my most cherished mentors, Mary Morrissey. I did some training with the Life Mastery Institute in California a couple years ago and these three little words were the missing key that I needed to really propel me into a way of living and being that I still had not experienced.

Mary Morrissey and Bob Proctor are two people who have been instrumental in me not only being who I am, but where I am in life, and I send them a great deal of gratitude.

Now I don't know who originally taught this to Mary, or if it was shared between her and Bob, but I always give recognition where recognition is due and I need you to know that this was not my solo creation. I learned from these two Masters and have since developed my own way of using this within my professional business practice.

I'd like to also add that as you use these 3 magic words, your life will actually begin to change. I always find it interesting when people say they want to change but then when it really starts happening they're shocked.

So how does it work?

First and foremost, in order to use these 3 magic words, you must become aware of a few key things. One of them being that there is an invisible side of life that is actually responsible for creating your visible, or material, side of life. That's right, we live in an inside-out universe. (This I also learned from Mary)

So what does that mean, the invisible side of life? It means that before something can happen in your external world like; shape shifting your body, writing that book, getting that new job, making more money, or having that relationship you've always wanted, you have to know that it's an inside out job.

Before anything can become a thing like the clothes you wear, the chair you sit in, the car you drive, or the business you operate they all started as a thought or a dream in someone's mind.

Try this on for size!

If I were to ask you to think of the Eiffel tower for a moment, you can picture the Eiffel tower in your mind, can't you? Perhaps you see it in the evening when it's lit up with lights, or perhaps you can see it in the daytime with blue skies abound. Either way, you can see a picture of it clearly in your mind.

Now, if I were to ask you to think of a blue shoe, a picture comes into your mind of a blue shoe, doesn't it? It could be your favorite runners, a pair of awesome heels, or something from when you were a child, but again, you can bring something to mind.

Now if I asked you to picture what the mind looks like, you might think of your brain and get an image of that, but that is not your mind. Your mind is actually something that is invisible. Thoughts are invisible; a dream is something that is invisible. There are invisible Universal laws that are flowing into your life right now, but how do you plug into them?

To expand on this, think about the law of electricity for a moment with me. The law of electricity is always working all of the time, but do you know how it actually works? Most of us have no idea how it works, I certainly didn't, but its something we plug into every single day of our lives. What we do know is that we can take a lamp, plug it in, and we get light.

Well, the law of electricity is also invisible, just like a radio station; there are certain wavelengths and frequencies that are invisible. Einstein, bless his soul, taught us that everything is energy, and I quote, "Everything is energy and that's all there is to it. Match the frequency to the reality you want and you cannot help but get that reality. It can be no other way. This is not Philosophy. This is Physics."

So when you jump into your vehicle and you put on the radio, if a song comes on that you don't really like, what do you do? You change the channel! You do this until you find a channel that resonates with you and you get a song that you like. You are quite literally matching the frequency to the reality, or in this case the song that you want to listen to, and this becomes your new reality.

Well, our lives work in a very similar way. The radio frequencies that we listen to are all functioning in an invisible manner and in our human lives we refer to them as thoughts. We don't see our thoughts, we can't touch them, but we all know how impactful they are in our lives.

Our thoughts come into our mind and we end up attaching onto whichever one has been hanging around in there the longest (think radio station, which stations are you listening to?), and that invisible thought frequency sends a wavelength through our physical body and out into our external, or material world. It acts like a magnet to attract to us more of what we are thinking about, or in this case, the channel we are listening to.

So, if we are constantly listening to the radio station of fear as an example, we attract to us, like a magnet, more of the same. Quite literally, what you focus on expands. In essence, we take an invisible thought like fear and we attract to ourselves more visible experiences in our lives that will reaffirm more fear.

If we are tuned into the radio station called stress, anxiousness, and overwhelm - we will energetically attract to us more experiences in our visible, external world, to reaffirm that we get more stress, anxiousness, and overwhelm.

So just like how you would change the dial to select a different song on the radio, you can also choose your thoughts so that they become an outward reflect of your hearts deepest desires.

It's all about energy my friend, and it's all about 'what are you focusing on' when it comes to the thoughts that are running your life right now.

The problem is that nobody tells you this stuff!

They don't tell you that you also have a certain individualized frequency that is unique to you, and that it radiates from the inside out. It is your Soul Frequency, or vibration, and it too is invisible to the human eye so you end up not believing in it.

They don't tell you that your life is governed largely by your mind, particularly your subconscious mind, and that you can actually reprogram what channel, or song, is playing in there to change what your life is like, in all areas, should you choose to.

So earlier when I asked you to picture the mind, what I have been illustrating to you is that there really is no picture that 'comes to mind'. What you do need to know, for now, is that you have a conscious and a subconscious mind.

And of the two, it is the subconscious mind that is really responsible for holding the frequency of who you are, what your beliefs are, and what invisible energetic frequencies you are sending out into your visible world.

If you live your life and never reflect upon or exam what you have in your subconscious mind, you will constantly be asking the question of 'Why me?' and living from a victim mentality. You will continue to think that life is happening 'to' you, rather than acknowledging that you are a powerful creator and life is happening 'through' you. Should you choose to live here, that's totally cool, but if you're reading this book chances are you've already made your choice to move past this.

It is of high value to gain an understanding of how it is you're getting the results you're getting in life, whether you like them or not. *Up Until Now*, are the 3 magic words that are going to allow you to change the channel that you have been tuned into which has been bringing you the lack, limitation, stress, and fears that are keeping you stuck.

You are going to learn a whole new way of being able to attract to you the peace, calm confidence, happiness, and courage to really live the life you would love to be living right now.

But first, why is change so hard?

Notes

CHAPTER 5 - WHY IS CHANGE SO HARD?

"If you always do what you've always done, you always get what you've always gotten."

– Henry Ford

When someone is drawn to work with me, they have gotten to a point in their lives where they've tried everything and they've reached the end of their rope. They have the best intentions, they are dedicated, they are really making this a priority and yet they still aren't seeing the peace, prosperity, confidence or abundance that they desire.

Why is that?

I remember way back in the beginning when I knew I had to make some serious changes in my life and how hard that was for me because I was listening to a really old out-of-date radio station in my head that was not in alignment with where I was trying to go to.

I remember how dedicated I had to be, how much willpower it took, how repetition was the key to making the new positive habits in my life, and how I had to really be mindful of what I was thinking and giving my energy to.

So do you remember that whole conscious and subconscious mind thing? Good! Because when we are young and just coming into this world we only have a subconscious mind. Our conscious mind hasn't really come into play yet.

So imagine an open container with an endless bottom and no lid. That is your subconscious mind as a young child. Now think of the lid as being a filter, but because there is no lid on this container anything and everything that is going on around you gets dumped into the container.

So as we are growing and living our lives as infants we only have this subconscious part of the mind, which is totally open, acting like a sponge absorbing the beliefs systems, habits, patterns, and stories of the people closest to us.

With the accumulation and repetition of many years of input we literally end up adopting our parents' beliefs. We adopt the beliefs of our cultural upbringing; our religious upbringing, our educational system, what we repeatedly see and hear from marketing and advertising, and any other impactful events that may have taken place in our lives.

What this also means is that your current reality in life now is a perfect outer reflection of your inner thoughts and paradigms. You'll recall that we live in an inside out Universe so in order to change what's happening in your life externally you have to change what is going on in the inside first, and that begins with your thoughts.

Let me take you a little deeper into this whole paradigm thing!

Your paradigms are the old set of beliefs, habits and stories that are currently operating from your subconscious mind, whether you like it or not. Say you grew up constantly hearing beliefs like; life is hard, money doesn't grow on trees, you'll never amount to anything, you don't have what it takes, you're crazy to think you can do that, and this world is out to get you.

You can imagine how different of a life you would be living if you grew up hearing these beliefs instead; you can do anything you put your mind to, you are beautiful, you are loved, life is meant to be fun, face your fears, and don't let anybody ever tell you that you can't do something!

Makes sense doesn't it?

Now, you may have the best intentions to want to live a financially abundant life, with a partner who loves and honors you, with a career that you absolutely adore, and in a body that is healthy and full of vitality and strength. But! If your paradigms are the opposite to all of this and you subconsciously believe that having money makes you bad, you're not good enough or lovable, you can't do what you love because you're afraid it won't bring you money, and your body will always be overweight and tired, you can see where the disconnect happens.

Your paradigms are similar to that of a thermostat in your home. (This is actually a pretty cool way to learn how paradigms work). When you set the thermostat in your home to a certain number the house temperature isn't going to be able to go past the number that you set it to. This ensures that the house is always at a comfortable level.

So we all have these thermostatic settings that are keeping us living inside our comfort zones where we're not able to sustain lasting change when we venture out above the level that we're set to.

And again, these thermostatic settings have been with us since a very young age and we all have different settings when it comes to the many areas in our lives, like; health, finances, relationships, love, time & money freedom, career, and how we create and express ourselves.

They have been programmed in our subconscious minds from the time we were infants, and they become our way of thinking, acting, living, and behaving in our current present day reality.

Think of it this way, if you had a brand new computer and you tried to install an operating system on this new computer from 10, 20 or 30 years ago, do you think you would get the best results from that computer in today's world. That's easy, we all know the answer to this is a whopping No.

So imagine living your life this way. Here you are as this brand new computer and yet you're trying to live a life based on an old outdated operating system that was given to you years ago, that wasn't even yours. They were never your beliefs; they belonged to everyone and everything else around you and you just happened to absorb them into your existence like a sponge.

And any time you try to do something different that causes you to step above the current set point of your old paradigm, or belief system, it is going to want to pull you back down into your comfort zone because you haven't been taught how to adjust the setting.

As an example, I get a lot of people who come to me in a business capacity all of the time that want to make more money. Let's say that they're currently making $100,000 a year but they want to be making $200 000 or $300 000 a year. Anytime they get close to these higher figures they find that they sabotage themselves. They do something unconsciously to kill a deal, they end up getting sick, they hurt themselves, or they end up getting some kind of expense that swallows up a bunch of the money that would have taken them closer to their goal. So what they haven't known, *Up Until Now*, is that their money paradigm, or thermostatic setting, is still back at that old lower number.

They actually have old paradigms that they don't even know exist and when we start uncovering what they are, they sound something like this: If I make more money than my spouse she/he will leave me, having too much money means I am a bad person, I can't be a spiritual person and make a lot of money, when I was a child I was never good with money and no one trusted me with it, so I don't trust myself or know how to invest & save for a rainy day, money has always been a struggle for me.

So you can see how these paradigms, or set points, would actually keep these people living small. They keep all of us living small and they keep us living in a victim mentality which then keeps us stuck in the same old rut year after year not able to make lasting change even though we have the best intentions to do so.

So here you are, present day and time, living your life trying to fit into this world and please everyone around you, and do all the right things when you pick up this book, and you realize, 'Hey, is this even really me? Is what I'm doing even really what I want to be doing with my life? Who Am I?'

Stay with me, you're doing great!

What I've learned over the years is that our paradigms are sneaky little things that can delay us in ways where we end up saying to ourselves, 'ow, I'll just do that later. I'll do something about my health, or my finances, or my relationship later' and days turn into weeks turn into months and before you know it another year has passed by and you are sitting back, shaking your head, wondering why you didn't accomplish the things that were important to you.

Paradigms are a huge part of why change is so hard, and if you don't know that you have them it's like walking uphill in sand; yeah, not fun! Every time you try to make a positive change and go above that thermostatic setting your paradigm pulls you back down.

For the majority of people in the world, we have never looked inside ourselves long enough to question whether what we believe and how we're living is true for us. Do you know what's true for you? Do you know what you believe and what you don't believe based purely on your heart and not on everybody else? I certainly didn't until I was pushed to the edge and had to reevaluate how I was living my life.

What is your belief system around money and finances? What is your current set point when it comes to relationships, love and self-worth? What do you believe about your health and your body? What's your belief system around your business or your company?

Do you believe that you are worthy of having a beautiful and prosperous life? Is it possible for you to change what your body looks like on the inside and the outside?

What are your daily habits like? Are they healthy for you? Do they align with your Soul's purpose? Again, when you look at your current external results in life, they are going to be a perfect reflection of your internal paradigms and will help you to answer these questions.

We have all heard of the comfort zone. Well, your paradigms all live within, and around the edges of, your comfort zone. The moment you try to do something different, drive home a new way, go somewhere that you've never been before, your paradigms jump up and let you know that you're getting close to the edge of your comfort zone.

So here's the good news my dear: WE CAN CHANGE THEM! Wahooo.

Yes, it's true! And before I help you do this you have got to know that it is no one's fault that you have these paradigms. I want to be very clear around this because the victim mentality will want to react and blame everyone and everything for why its life is the way it is, and I'm here to remind you that that is not true.

Sweetheart, this is just part of the dance of life. It is no one's fault! So if you think that by blaming your parents, friends, institutions, schools, governments, or anything else that you will be helping yourself, you will actually be hurting yourself even more.

You've got to understand that your parents were doing the best that they could do with what they had at the time. Remember, they too were once a young child who had a similar experience to you where they adopted the beliefs, habits, stories and patterns of their parents, environments, and life events.

So there is no one to blame here. It simply 'Is What It Is' and the more you can see this from the perceptive of the souls evolution the easier it will be to move forward in your life. As a Soul, we recognize that through contrast we are going to better remember who we are. By having experiences that are 'not' in alignment with us, we can then better navigate and make choices as to 'what is' in alignment with us.

So the first step to changing paradigms and living your life in the way you know you want to be is by acknowledging that you actually do have these little darlings. When you bring your awareness to the patterns and belief systems in your life right now, then you can begin to start living your life by design rather than by default.

Here are some of the most common paradigms that I get from people on a daily basis:

I'm not good enough,

I don't know how,

I'm not smart enough,

I don't have the business sense,

I don't have the schooling behind me,

I don't trust myself,

I'm not good with money,

I'm afraid of what other people will think of me,

I'm just not lucky in life,

I always get the shitty end of the stick,

He/She will never go for me; I'm not their type,

I'm un-lovable,

I can't do this it's too hard,

It's too late for me,

I'm a failure,

I'm afraid of success,

I'm afraid to be judged,

Nothing ever works out for me so why even try.

Sound familiar?

And this is just the tip of the iceberg. If yours isn't on that list don't go getting all 'smug' on me now and racing into that ego of yours thinking you're all that and a bag of chips.

We all have them in the different areas of our lives, even you my dear;)!

The next step is to honor that if you were able to change all on your own, don't you think you would have done it by now?

Here's the thing. If it were easy to change on our own then you would never be reading a book like this now would you? Stress wouldn't bother you; fear would be a thing of the past and anxiety? - what anxiety!

What ends up happening for most people is that they venture out on their own with the best of intentions and very quickly they find themselves sabotaging their progress and falling back into their self-limiting beliefs, old paradigms, and comfort zones. (Which, by the way, aren't really all that comfortable, they're just familiar!)

Now good hearted people don't mean to do this, they don't want to do this, but they cannot see their own subconscious blocks and so they don't know how to keep going when their old paradigm tries to pull them back down.

So, my dear sweet soul! You have got to know that you are limitless. You are timeless. You can do anything that you set your mind to and then take bold courageous action steps towards.

The only restrictions that you put on yourself come from within you, and they start with your invisible thoughts.

By gaining a better understanding of paradigms and how they are running your life it kind of makes sense that changing on your own, without the proper support or structure, rarely works in the long term.

Think about top athletes, or celebrities, or successful business owners for a moment. We hire top coaches, mentors, and consultants to help us maintain a structure of support and help us with these subconscious blocks so that we get out of our comfort zone and over to where the magic happens.

I think you've been hanging out in that old comfort zone long enough don't you?

It's time for you to fly!

Notes

CHAPTER 6 - PLACING YOUR ORDER

"You cannot get to your dream, you must come from it. And in order to come from it, you must become it.

– Mary Morrissey

When we are attaching onto an old paradigm like 'I'm not good enough', as an example, and we accept that old thought and stay tuned into its frequency it goes from our conscious mind, down into our subconscious mind, and then sends a vibration out through our bodies signaling to the universe that we'd like more of that.

Imagine walking into a restaurant and taking a seat. The server approaches the table and you can see that his/her nametag reads, 'The Universe". You would think twice before placing your order, wouldn't you? I know I would.

Life is just like that! We get so comfortable ordering the same food, the same drink, and the same dessert over and over again and then we complain when it shows up on our table. It is your subconscious mind, where the paradigms are hanging out, that is placing the order to your server, 'The Universe".

Now the server, or in our case "The Universe" doesn't care what you order. It's just going to go put your order in and wait for the kitchen to prepare it and then bring it back out for you to enjoy.

So how do you know what you're ordering? That's easy! Pay attention to what you are focusing on.

Are you so focused on how stressed and overwhelmed you are that you keep talking to everyone about it, and then unconsciously order more of that?

Are you so stuck in fear and afraid to do anything that you keep ordering that?

Or, are you ordering more side plates of 'I'm not good enough' 'This will never work' and 'Nothing good ever comes my way'? Yuk, could you imagine what those dishes would taste like? No thanks!

You would never consciously order that up from the Universe! Yet it's what I see people do every day because no one has taught them that they actually have the power to choose what thoughts get to stay and what thoughts get to go when it comes to their own minds.

If you keep focusing on, 'I'm so stressed, there isn't enough time in the day, and I don't know what to do'. You guessed it, you will keep attracting to yourself more situations and circumstances to reaffirm that you are: stressed out, don't have time, and don't know what to do.

Think back to the radio station analogy, just because you've been listening to an old station doesn't mean you have to anymore.

You have the power to go ahead and tune into another frequency at any time. Instead of listening to the 'lack, limitation, and scarcity' channel, you can plug yourself into the 'abundance, gratitude, and joy' channel. The choice is always yours.

Notes

CHAPTER 7 - PLUGGING BACK IN

"It doesn't matter where you are, you are nowhere compared to where you can go."

– Bob Proctor

I am reminded of a story that came to me through a teaching from OSHO many years ago in one of his books, and although I don't recall which book it is, the story illustrates my point here beautifully.

Here's the story as I remember it:

"There was a young boy and his mother who lived in a beautiful garden. The garden was so extraordinarily beautiful that people from near and far traveled each year to see the flowers and admire the beauty. One year, the mother became sick and had to leave the house and the garden, and her young son was left to take care of everything.

The young boy cared for the garden and worked from sun up to sun down every day. Roughly a month's time had passed and his mother returned home. As she got better and had more strength to walk she went outside to see how everything was looking in the garden.

Seeing the condition of the garden, she was shocked. All of the plants and flowers were withered up, ready to die, and falling to the earth. She beckoned for her son and said, "What did you do while I was away? All the flowers are just about dead!"

The son started to cry because every day he had worked so hard in the garden kissing all of the flowers and singing to them. He would wipe the dust from each and every leaf and flower petal, and yet he too was concerned because the flowers kept drying up and dying.

As the boy told his mother this, she said "Ow my dear boy, you have yet to learn that the life of the flowers is not in the flowers, and the life of the leafs is not in the leafs. The life of a plant is in a place that cannot be seen with your eyes."

I absolutely love this story because it illustrates the power that is in the invisible. As we grow in our human lives, we begin to understand that the life of the plant is in the roots, but until someone teaches us this and our awareness of this fact grows, we are naive and think that the life of the flower is in the flower just like the young boy.

You and I and the other 7.4 billion people on the planet get so caught up on the visible side of things that we forget where our life force energy comes from. It comes from the invisible side of life. You can call it whatever you want: The Universe, The Divine, Source, Infinite Intelligence, Great Spirit, The Creator, Life-force Primal Energy, God, Krishna, Alice, Mark or William. It doesn't matter what you call it, as long as you are aware of the 'something' that exists that is giving you and me our life-force energy too.

For many souls on the planet right now, they have forgotten about the invisible roots that feed their life. They are wandering around aimlessly trying to make sense of life and unintentionally cutting themselves off from their roots.

Do you remember in the first chapter of this book, I spoke about how we can know something, but that's not the same as actually applying it to our lives? Well, that's what *Up Until Now* can do for you. It's the practical application that will keep you plugged into the Universe (or whatever you want to call it) so that you can start to re-program the old operating system in your subconscious mind and allow you to wake up and start really being who you know you've always been.

So, what's next and why do you need to know it?

The next step is abundance! We live in an abundant Universe where everything and anything is possible for you. Now in the beginning, when I was waking up and learning this new way of life I didn't believe I lived in an abundant Universe. Are you kidding me? I thought how could there be abundance when all I ever see and hear about is lack, limitation, and scarcity.

It was many years before I had the revelation that we actually do live in an abundant universe and that the lack, scarcity, and limitation I had been witnessing and experiencing all those years were due largely to three main things; greed, a lack of distribution, and low levels of awareness. It actually had nothing to do with the Universe being abundant and had everything to do with how I was viewing, and perceiving, my life in the world.

You need to know this because when you start to tap into the truth that we live in this abundant universe, anything and everything is possible for you again.

And just like how you needed to know that we live in an inside out Universe, you also need to know that you are more than your body.

When you start to understand that you have a body, but you are not just your body, your life begins to change in a really fascinating and fun way. When you understand that your body is a gift, it's the vehicle, the vessel, the catalyst, the external body suit that your soul gets to wear so that you can hang out down here on earth; things begin to shift in a really beautiful way.

You actually want to start eating healthier energizing foods. You see the beauty in all of the scars, the weight, the curves, and the wrinkles in your body. You find beauty in your feet for having taken you everywhere you've been in life. You find beauty in your heart, even if it's been broken in the past, and you see how incredibly strong it is.

You want to naturally just be active and move your body in ways that allow it feel free. You dance, you sing, you run, you jump, you swim and you kick your feet up because you recognize what a gift it truly is.

You honor that there is a time for work and there is a time for play. You realize that rest is the only way for your system to recalibrate and you start saying no to the demands of the world, and yes to the much needed time and self-nurturing that you've been neglecting for yourself.

And the best part is nobody needs to tell you what to do or how to do it because you are now going to the roots and getting clear about what's important to you. When you do this, you tap into your internal body wisdom and you know exactly what to do for yourself and you start doing it no matter what anybody else thinks.

You'll get to a point in your life, in one aspect or another, where you'll say enough is enough and decide I'm not going to live like this anymore. That's where the magic starts to happen baby! So fun!

You say to yourself, *Up Until Now,* I have let stress run my life, *but now,* I choose peace.

Up Until Now, I was afraid to go to that dance class because I thought I had to lose a few pounds first, *but now,* I know that I deserve to dance if I want to and so I'm going to tell fear to take a back seat and I'm doing this thing!

Up Until Now, I thought I had to have it all figured out, *but now,* I know that the 'how' is up to the Universe. All I need to do is get clear about 'what' I want and who I am and let the universe provide the 'how' and meet me half way. I'm responsible for the 'what'; the Universe is responsible for the 'how'.

Up Until Now, I didn't think I could make money and take care of my living arrangements while doing what I love, *but now,* I know that where there's a will there's a way and I am going to expand my mind and ask the Universe for some help with new ideas to make this my reality.

Up Until Now, I thought that I had to push and force everything to come together in my life, *but now,* I know that the more I push and force something the more it's not for me. The things that are in alignment with me and that are on my Soul Frequency Channel are going to easily and naturally to me.

Up Until Now, I used to let stress and anxiety run my life, *but now,* I choose to release the stress, release the anxiety, and connect inside to my breath to help slow me down and ground myself.

Up Until Now, I used to always wait until I was sick before taking care of my health, *but now,* I am going to be more proactive in my life and start participating in alternative therapies and nutrition in order to stay balanced.

When you use *Up Until Now,* you are stopping that neurotransmitter in your brain from going down the old freeway that it's been going down for years. When you have the awareness and can catch yourself before you start into your old pattern and say, 'Whoa! Hang on here!' And you hit the Stop button – you are taking back control of your life and you are re-directing that neurotransmitter in your brain to a new location with a new positive uplifting message.

Doesn't that make you feel so friggin good? You bet it does! You get to take your power back and create your life!

Check this out!

Imagine that neurotransmitter has now come to a fork in the road by you hitting the Stop button and saying the 3 magic words *Up Until Now*. For years it has just gone to the right like an old song on repeat heading onto the highway, *but now*, you're going to direct it to the left by replacing that old outdated paradigm with something new and more empowering for yourself.

The old freeway is about to start getting less traffic as you repeatedly keep redirecting the new thought onto a brand new single-track trail. Eventually, this single track will become a two-way road, which over time will turn into a gravel road, which then will be paved, and you'll start to add more lanes to, and it will eventually become the new freeway that holds the new positive uplifting thought.

Out with the old and in with new as they say.

CHAPTER 8 - PLANTING THE SEED

"Change the way you see things and the things you see will change"

–Wayne Dyer

Research has shown that once we reach the approximate age of 7 years old we begin to form the conscious part of our mind. The lid that was never on the subconscious mind is now put on and it acts like a filter, and on top of it, we begin to form our conscious mind.

Let's have some fun with this!

Imagine that you are drawing a large circle on a piece of paper with a horizontal line going right through the middle of the circle splitting it in half. The upper portion is your conscious mind and the lower portion is your subconscious mind.

Now carry that horizontal line outside of the circle walls a little bit to the right and go ahead and draw a flower with the visible part of the flower on the upper half of that line, and the roots on the lower half. You can clearly see that the visible part of the flower relates to the conscious mind and the roots relate to the subconscious mind.

Pause the show!

(For the record, I'm using an illustration similar to the one I just asked you to imagine that came to me through Bob Proctors teachings. When I speak of the conscious and the subconscious mind, the information that I relay to you has partly come from Bob and I want to make note of that here. What an incredible teacher. Credits abound Bob Proctor!)

And we're back....

Ok. So as you go through life and attach onto the thoughts that you are thinking, they first come into your conscious mind at the top of the circle. From there, you have a choice to make as to what you are going to do with those thoughts because if you accept them they then transfer down and begin to grow in your subconscious mind, where the roots live.

Let me explain it to you this way!

When I was a little girl growing up on the farm I loved to spend time with my Poppa in his garden. I always asked to plant the seeds because I was fascinated that when I put the seed into the earth, within a short period of time, something would actually grow. If I took a carrot seed and placed it into the earth, a carrot would grow. If I took an onion seed and placed it into the earth, an onion would appear. It was the coolest thing and it blew my mind at the time to learn that the earth could grow all of these different seeds.

So imagine for a moment that you have some seeds in your hand right now. The seed in your left hand will grow a beautiful rose bush, and the seed in your right hand will grow a poisonous vine. As you plant both of those seeds at the same time into the earth, what does the earth have to do?

It has to grow both seeds.

Well, your thoughts are those seeds. You may have the thought in your conscious mind of 'I got this, this is easy' in your left hand, and a thought of 'I can't do it' in the right hand, but when you plant those thoughts into the subconscious mind it acts just like the earth. It will grow both of those thoughts just like it does with the seeds.

You see the earth is neutral. It will grow whatever you put into it. It doesn't get to kick out the poisonous seed and keep the rose bush. Just like your subconscious mind can't kick out the thought of 'I can't do it' and only focus on the thought of 'I got this, this is easy', it will simply grow whatever is being planted into it.

Remember the previous story about the boy and the garden? Well, your subconscious mind is where the roots of those thoughts live and they spread out into your life. As the energy from the roots of that thought spreads, it also comes out and through your body sending out into the Universe a vibration that signals for you to attract, like a magnet, more of that same energy.

Now we live in a world that loves to give a great amount of attention to the flower because it is visible, but it forgets all about the roots. It usually takes us having to hit rock bottom somewhere questioning why we're not happy to remember that if we had just tended to the roots in the first place, the flower would have naturally taken care of itself.

Here's a perfect example to illustrate this:

Our stomach hurts, we take a pill. That doesn't seem to work, so we try a different pill. All of a sudden we get a rash, so we go see our Doctor who gives us another prescription for another kind of pill. Oopsies!

Now we have to take something on top of that last one because of the side effects it causes and we can no longer go into the sun (which by the way, is our life-force energy and greatly needed in our lives. Period!) We develop acne, we get IBS, we start getting headaches, we start gaining weight, we get depressed because of our excess weight gain and the vicious cycle begins all over again as we now try to numb ourselves out and find distractions that will help us from not having to feel anything because of all the Band-Aids we've been trying to use instead of going straight to the root of the problem in the first place.

This is what is happening all over our world. We have been giving all of our attention to the external; the house, the body, the job, the car, the clothes, and we have been giving no attention to the inside. To the roots, our heart, our soul, our spirit, our thoughts, and our dreams.

If we constantly keep trying to brush the dust off the flower, and never deal with the roots, we will eventually wither up; not just physically but also emotionally, mentally, spiritually, relationally, financially, energetically, etc.

So the amazing part here is that you have a choice. Scream it from the rooftops would ya! Be an active participant in your life, because as long as you're breathing you're creating a life for yourself.

You can choose whether you're going to live your life based on the circumstances, situations, and events outside of yourself or you can take yourself from the victim to the victor, and start creating your life by design in a way that really feels good to you.

As Ghandi once said, "You can't change how people treat you or what they say about you. All you can do is change how you react to it."

Having the free will and being able to choose how you want to respond to a situation or circumstance is one of the best parts of this human experience. Notice I did not use the word react, I am carefully choosing to use the word respond. There is a big difference.

A reaction is that knee-jerk thing that happens and it comes straight from the land of the paradigm. It is that old outdated reaction that you habitually have done for years. A response is when you mindfully choose how you would like to deal with any given situation because you know you have a choice.

And not only do you get to choose how you respond in your life, the other amazing truth is that you are not defined by your past or your history.

The difference is that you 'have' a past and you 'have' a history, but they are not who you are today. They are simply old stories that you forgot to flip the page on.

Just because you have been living your life a certain way, *Up Until Now*, does not mean that you have to continue down that same old path if you don't want to. Every day is a new day in the book of your life, and only you get to decide how you're going to write your new story moving forward.

I've heard it said that "Some people will live 100 years, and other people will live 1 year 100 times." Which one will it be for you? It's time to decide.

Notes

CHAPTER 9 - THE GREEN LIGHT

"You can't depend on your eyes when your imagination is out of focus."

- Mark Twain

Up Until Now will work on any old paradigm that you have kickin' around in that subconscious mind of yours, but the three main ones I have chosen to focus on here are the ones around fear, stress and anxiety.

These three experiences go hand in hand and have some of the deepest roots that I've seen in many people's lives all around the world no matter what you do for a living.

Allow me to demonstrate.

We are afraid to do something because we have a fear of failure and we don't want to be ridiculed, but because we don't ever do anything different we keep getting the same old results in life that we don't want in the first place. This leads us to experiencing more stress. The fear keeps us stuck, our external results don't every change, this frustrates us, and then our stress level starts to get up into the red as we worry about how we are ever going to do the things we want to do. Once our stress level skyrockets, the anxiety kicks in and we start the patterns all over again.

The anxiousness leads to more fear, the fear leads to more stress, and the stress leads to more anxiety. Yikes!! I remember living my life this way and it was not fun.

You see, the stress, fear, and anxiety that you're experiencing are just symptoms of your paradigms. They are the visible (or flower portion) of what you're experiencing and what your human body is relaying to you, but they are not the root cause. The root cause is the underlying old belief, thought pattern, or habit sitting in your subconscious mind. A usual suspect if often the paradigm that sounds like, 'I'm not good enough!' When you believe this to be true you begin to attract experiences into your life that reflect, 'I'm not good enough' and the fear, stress and anxiety continually show up. You stress about what other people think, you're anxious of making a mistake because you secretly feel like you're not good enough, and then fear not succeeding at whatever it is you're attempting to be, do, or have. Make sense? You're so awesome!

So as you start to live your life more authentically and begin to look at the beliefs, habits, and stories (or songs, remember the radio analogy) that keep playing in your subconscious mind, you're going to use the 3 magic words to start tuning into the channel and the frequency that is more in alignment with you and your Souls purpose so that you can change those old paradigms.

So how do you know what your Soul true purpose is? That's easy, you look at two main things in your life. Where's the pleasure and where's the pain? Where are my longings/ desires and where is my discontent/unhappiness?

Ask yourself the following questions:

What am I passionate about?

What lights me up?

What are my desires, yearnings, and longings?

What do I really want? - And don't come from the place of, 'what do you think you can have?', or 'what do you think you can do based on the past?' really ask yourself - what do I really truly want out of my life?

Also, look at the opposite side and ask yourself:

What's not working out very well for me?

Where's the discontent or unhappiness in my life?

What area(s) of my life do I feel need some love?

Most people know what they don't want but they have no idea what they really do want because they haven't been putting their focus or energy there.

This is where you want to invite your inner child to come out and play to help you remember what it's like to dream again. What it's like to use your imagination.

By the way, our imagination is also invisible just like our mind, our thoughts, and our dreams. Without our imagination we have nothing! Without our imagination, we are a sailboat out to sea with no wind to take us anywhere. It is by far one of the most important mental faculties that we have access to 24/7 and yet we rarely use it.

As children, we used our imaginations all of the time in everything that we did. Trust me, growing up with younger siblings on a farm and playing outside was the absolute best place for us because it created a beautiful canvas for us to use our imaginations on a daily basis.

This world is your canvas; your life is a book with pages that have yet to be written and you are the author. The chapters from your past and your history, you don't see them anymore, we've already turned the page on them.

In front of you, is a blank page, use your imagination and dream big so that you can write the new story that is coming straight from that real authentic beautiful person we call YOU! Your new story may be hidden behind a mask, it may be pushed back in the corner of your heart because you haven't been spending much time there lately, or it may be a little dusty, but it's in there!

And honey! It's just waiting for you to give it the green light!

Notes

CHAPTER 10 – COMING ALIVE

"Opportunity dances with those already on the dance floor"

– Unknown

Have you ever walked down the sidewalk and noticed the small blades of grass growing up from underneath the cement? Or seen the picture of the trees that grow upside down out of rock and then curve back up in order to grow towards the sunlight?

If that tiny blade of grass can push up through the cement seeking to find the light, and that bold tree can grow from a tiny seed up through that hard rock, you can most definitely change your life.

The same energy that lives and breathes the tiny blade of grass, and the tree, is the same energy that is living and breathing in you and I. Did you know that we don't even breathe ourselves? We are actually being breathed! Even right now as you read these pages you aren't thinking to yourself, 'hey, am I breathing?' No, you just breathe.

When you are driving your car down the road, talking on your Bluetooth, drinking your coffee, changing lanes, watching the traffic, and trying to eat (which, for the record, I am not recommending that you do) your not thinking about breathing. Again, it is already naturally being done for you.

You can bring your awareness to your breath and you can witness it, but it is through the Universal Life-force Energy that lives and breathes all things that you are being breathed and given life. So I'll say it again, if that tiny blade of grass can press up through the cement towards the light, you have the power to change your life into anything you want it to be. The only person stopping you; is you!

We are always amazed at nature, and how trees can grow out of rock faces and yet when it comes to our lives we are the first to forget that if it's possible for the tree, it has got to be possible for you and me.

The great news is that you now have a much clearer picture of how change is possible for you and how important it is to be mindful of the thoughts you are deciding to accept into your subconscious mind. You have taken the first bold step when it comes to living from the invisible side of life. As you become more and more aware of the Universal Life Force Energy breathing you, day in and day out, you will start to feel a sense of magic and hope in your life once again.

I am here to remind you that the Universal has got your back and it wants you to succeed. It wants you to live with courage, passion, unconditional love, a sense of security and safety knowing that you are enough, you are possible, and you are worthy of reaching the highest places in your heart and becoming the person you know you've always wanted to be.

When you know that the power within you is greater than anything going on outside of you and that the Universe has your back, you're more willing to take action steps into the direction of your future, instead of steps backwards into your old past and history.

Think of it like this.

The Universe acts like an invisible staircase. Once you've lived a little while and done some things in your life, made some choices, can you see the stairs under your feet behind you. It's easy to go backwards in life because it's easy to do the same things you've always done and look back to see the stairs.

It's not always easy to take a step forward when you can't even see the outline of a stair in the staircase. When you put *Up Until Now* into action in your life and you start taking that forward moving step up the staircase, with a dash of faith and a touch of trust, the staircase will begin to appear for you. The invisible side of life you feel with your heart, it's not always logical, but you know it's right.

So be sure to use *Up Until Now* in any way that feels good to you and help re-train your mind so that it's operating and vibrating at a higher frequency. Remember that what you continually focus upon, talk about, blog about, gossip about, watch on television, and write about will continue to expand and draw more of the same back to you.

When it comes to understanding energy, let's remember that 'Like' energy attracts 'Like' energy. Wherever you put your intention, your attention will follow. So I invite you to place it on the thoughts that are going to bring you more peace, more happiness, more prosperity, more love, and more joy than ever before.

As I've demonstrated all throughout this book, the basic layout for using the 3 magic words always remains the same.

One - Recognize the old paradigm is about to go on and repeat that old song.

Two - Take a deep breath to help center yourself and hit the Stop Button.

Three - Use the 3 Magic Words:

Up Until Now I used to (insert the old paradigm, reaction, limiting belief, habit, or pattern) ***but now*** I choose to (insert the new, positive, more empowering belief to replace the old one)

It's that simple. In less than 10 seconds, you've shifted your frequency from that old vibration/reaction, and tuned into a new channel! Job Well Done!

The key is to use it!

Make it a part of your everyday life. Write it down on a sticky note, put these words as a screen saver on your phone to remind yourself that you have a choice.

You are not the person who you once were; you are way more than that. Give yourself permission to move forward, give yourself permission to spread your wings and fly again.

The source of the happiness that you've been looking for is in your mind dear friend. Your freedom is in your mind, your peace is in your mind, your health is in your mind, and your abundance is in your mind first. They all begin as invisible things before they can become visible in your material, external, world.

With the energy coming to you from these pages, and the high level of awareness that you have just given yourself access to, your time has now arrived.

Embrace your heart! Change your channel! Tune into your unique frequency! Tend to your roots! Honor your desires and longings! Be curious towards the things that come naturally to you, and above all: **Love** yourself!

Take a chance. Do something different. There will never be another soul like you. Just like how your fingerprint is totally unique to you, you are here for a purpose and a reason, and when you start living from the truth of who you know you really are, only then will your gifts and talents start to come forth in ways that you didn't even know existed.

Get into alignment with your new frequency by turning the page on the old story of who you thought you were, and start living with the courage in your soul of who you know you truly are.

Up Until Now, you have been living your life a certain way, *but now*, you know that you, and you alone, have the power to change it.

Up Until Now, you have been afraid to be yourself, *but now*, you know that by not being authentic and real you are hurting yourself.

Up Until Now, you thought you only got one crack at this thing called life, *but now*, you know that at any time you have the ability to do the things you once thought were impossible.

Up Until Now, you didn't know how much your paradigms affected your life, *but now*, you do! And from here on out you have a life changing world-class tool to help you write your new story.

Stop worrying about what other people are going to think about you and start living your life. If you don't think you have what it takes, think again! All it takes is one small step after the other and you don't have to do it alone. This book has been your first step. Congratulations!

When you're ready to take the next one, you let me know.

I am here to support and serve you along your journey, and

I would love to hear from you. Feel free to contact me: meagan@meaganmckerroll.com so that we can assist you in learning the 'invisible side of life'.

Another way to keep raising your vibration and taking action steps is to register for my FREE teaching segment on the 2016 Global Transformation Summit where I am featured as one of the 'Hidden Teachers' from around the world: https://www.thetransformationsummit.live/a/1511/FEkZPfWa

I have dearly loved our time together and I look forward to spending more time with you again in the near future. I'd like to leave you with a quote that I live my life by in hopes that it will inspire and ignite the flame within your heart; it comes to you from Howard Thurman.

He says, *"Don't ask what the world needs, asks what makes you comes alive and go do it, because what the world needs is people who have come alive."*

It's time for you to turn the page, write your new story, and come alive!

You always have a choice! I Believe in YOU!

Wishing you Love Always & In All Ways.

Peace & Blessings

Namaste ~ Meagan

ABOUT THE AUTHOR

Meagan McKerroll is a #1 Best Selling Author, Teacher, Intuitive Healer, Licensed Holistic Health Practitioner (LHHP), and globally recognized Speaker who holds a Bachelors of Metaphysical Science (B.Msc).

This one-of-a-kind genuine free spirit is a compassionate and warm-hearted professional who is a forward thinking leader blessed to have studied with world-renowned experts in the fields of transformation, personal growth, spiritual consciousness, and awakening.

Meagan has made it her lifelong mission to 'Ignite The Human Spirit' in the hearts and minds of millions of people around the world, as she helps awaken you to the 'Invisible Side of Life'. By plugging you back into your authentic self and guiding you to have high-level frequency shifts, you will once again begin to live in alignment with your Soul's truth, purpose, and passion.

All of her work is created to assist you with activating and raising your vibration & frequency to bring you into your next level of becoming. She is considered to be a world-class mentor and teacher to open-minded individuals who are ready to take a quantum leap into the next chapter of their lives.

She is an advocate for; freedom, nature, consciousness, equality, living from the heart, and continuous life-long learning. To work with Meagan and participate in her life changing programs and services, you'll want to visit here website: www.meaganmckerroll.com

61913999R00051

Made in the USA
Charleston, SC
30 September 2016